THIS NOTEBOOK BELONGS TO: